STEP INTO SCIENCE

ROCKS AND SOIL

PETER RILEY

Enslow PUBLISHING

Published in 2025 by Enslow Publishing, LLC
2544 Clinton Street
Buffalo, NY 14224

First published in Great Britain in 2022 by Hodder & Stoughton

The text in this book was previously published in the series *Moving Up with Science*.

To my granddaughter, Holly Jane.

Editor: Elise Short
Design and Illustration: Collaborate Ltd

Manufactured in the United States of America

CPSIA compliance information: Batch #CW25ENS: For further information contact Enslow Publishing LLC, New York, New York at 1-800-398-2504.

Please visit our website, www.enslowpublishing.com. For a free color catalog of all our high-quality books, call toll free 1-800-398-2504 or fax 1-877-980-4454.

Cataloging-in-Publication Data

Names: Riley, Peter.
Title: Rocks and soil / Peter Riley.
Description: Buffalo, NY : Enslow Publishing, 2025. | Series: Step into science | Includes glossary and index.
Identifiers: ISBN 9781978541597 (pbk.) | ISBN 9781978541603 (library bound) | ISBN 9781978541610 (ebook)
Subjects: LCSH: Rocks--Juvenile literature. | Soils--Juvenile literature.
Classification: LCC QE432.2 R55 2025 | DDC 552--dc23

Find us on

We recommend adult supervision at all times while doing the activities in this book. Also, please be sure to do the following before starting an activity in which they are applicable (not all safety tips will apply to all activities):

- Wear an apron and cover surfaces.
- Tie back long hair.
- Ask an adult for help with cutting.
- Check materials for allergens.

CONTENTS

ROCKS IN SPACE

Earth is a rocky planet, but where did the rocks come from?

HOW EARTH BEGAN

Around 4.6 **billion** years ago, a cloud of **gas** and dust swirled around in space. The gases and dust formed a **star**—our Sun. The leftover **particles** formed **gravel**-sized pieces of rock.

These small pieces came together to form boulder-sized lumps of rock. These kept getting bigger and bigger until, after millions of years, Earth was formed. This is also how the other rocky **planets**—Mercury, Venus, and Mars—were formed.

EQUIPMENT:

- 10 tiny balls of modeling clay
- 10 medium-sized balls of modeling clay, 10 times larger than the tiny balls
- 10 large balls of modeling clay, 10 times larger again

Try the following experiment to see how a cloud of dust can make a rocky planet.

1 Add the 10 tiny balls together to make one ball, then add this ball to one of the medium-sized balls. Add this ball to all the other 9 medium-sized balls.

2 Add the ball they make to one of the large balls. Add all the large balls together to make your model planet.

ASTEROID BELT

Some lumps of rock stopped coming together and made **asteroids**. Asteroids form a huge belt around the rocky planets.

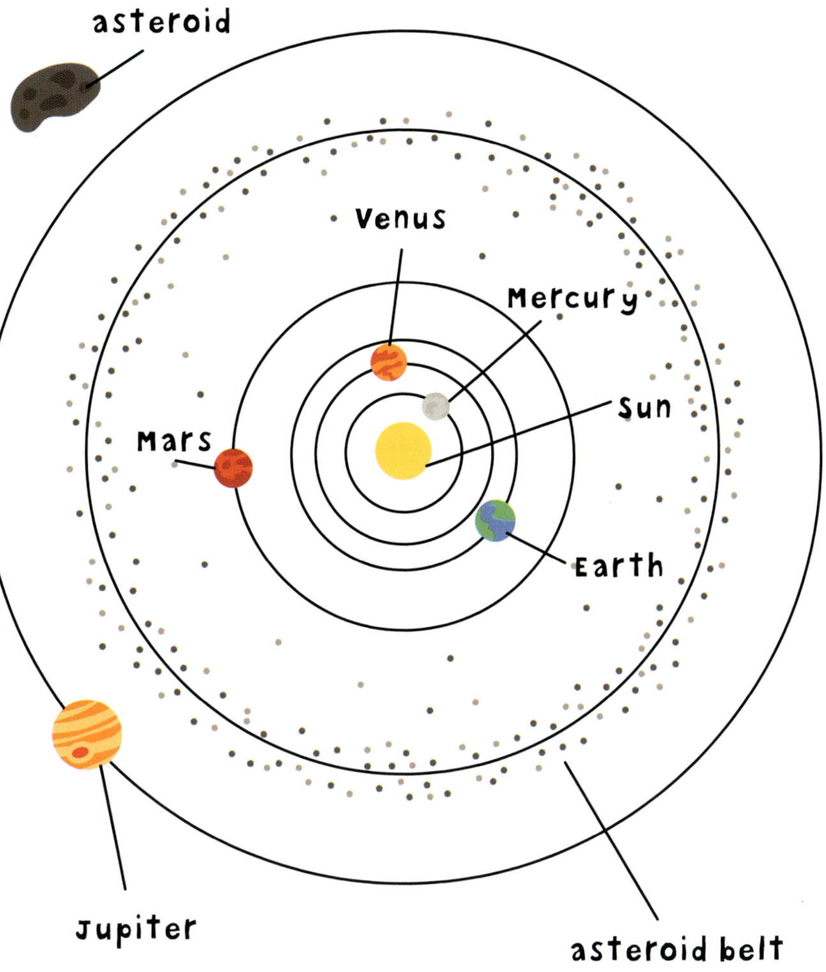

OTHER PLANETS

Beyond the asteroid belt, lumps of rocks formed the center of other planets in our **solar system**: Jupiter, Saturn, Uranus, and Neptune. These planets have **liquids** and gases around their rocky centers. Many planets have **moons** around them. These are also made of rock.

WHERE DO YOU FIND ROCKS IN THE SOLAR SYSTEM?

INSIDE THE EARTH

If you could slice open Earth, you would find it has four main parts. The part which forms the surface is called the crust. Beneath this is the mantle, and below the mantle are the outer core and inner core.

DIFFERENT LAYERS

The inner core is made from a huge metal ball that spins in the outer core liquid. The outer core is made from very hot liquid metal. Earth's mantle is made of hot rock, but the rock does not stay still. It moves very slowly under Earth's crust.

Scientists believe the hot rock of the mantle moves like toothpaste when you slowly squeeze it from a tube.

EARTH'S MOVING CRUST

Earth's crust is made from a few huge slabs of rock called tectonic plates. They make up the land and the floors of the seas. As the mantle moves, it makes the slabs in the crust move. When the edges of the slabs rub together they make the crust shake. This is what causes earthquakes. The slab of crust you are on now is moving very slowly.

This world map shows the blue outlines of tectonic plates. Some of the major ones are labeled.

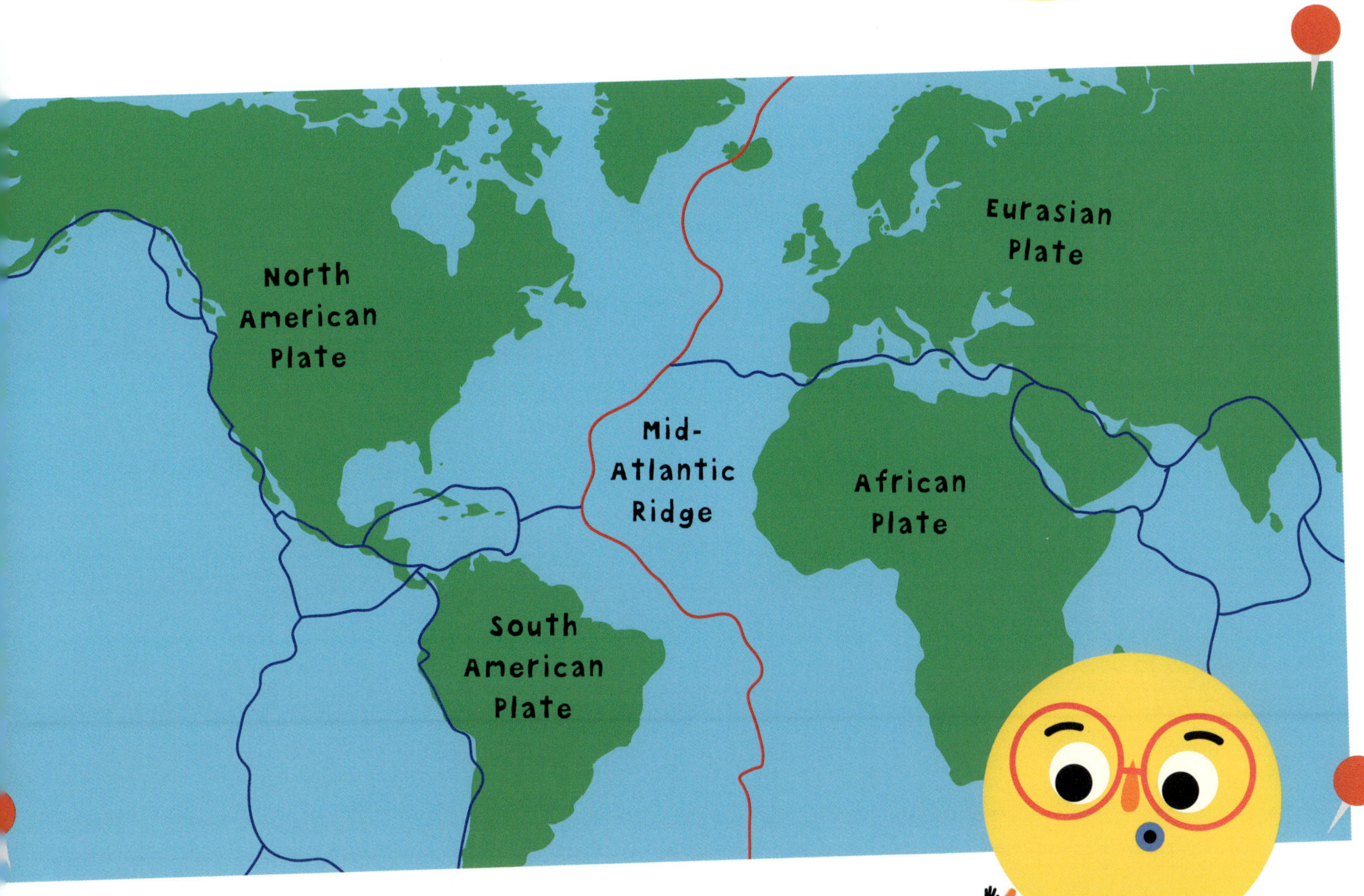

VOLCANOES

The rock in Earth's mantle is much hotter than the rock in the crust. In some places, the hot mantle rock, called magma, pushes up through cracks in the crust at a volcano. Two types of volcanoes are shield volcanoes and cone-shaped volcanoes.

SHIELD VOLCANOES

When a shield volcano **erupts**, the magma flows out and forms a liquid rock called **lava**. This cools down to make solid rock. The lava flows quickly and travels for long distances before it cools. This gives shield volcanoes gently sloping sides.

CONE-SHAPED VOLCANOES

Underneath a cone-shaped volcano, the magma builds up until it forces itself out in a great explosion. The erupting volcano shoots gases, steam, ash, and large rocks, called volcanic bombs, high into the air. The steam, ash, and gases form a cloud that settles over the land, while lava flows out of the top of the cone. When this lava cools, down it forms solid rock that often has steep sides.

SOIL FROM VOLCANIC ROCK

Some volcanoes have not erupted for a long time. They are called **extinct** volcanoes. Over thousands of years, the rocks from the volcanoes break down to make a rich soil that farmers use to grow their crops.

IGNEOUS ROCK

Igneous rock is made from the magma under Earth's crust. When a volcano erupts, the magma becomes lava, which flows away from the volcano and begins to cool. When lava cools, it forms rock with small **grains**. Basalt is the most common of these kinds of rocks.

GRANITE

Magma comes up through cracks in Earth's crust, but does not always reach the surface. It can stay in the crust and cool down slowly to form rocks with **crystals**. These crystals are much larger than the grains in basalt. **Granite** is a common example of a rock that forms in this way.

Over millions of years, rain, the Sun, and wind wear away the crust above the granite, and the rock reaches Earth's surface. It can form hills and mountains where the surrounding land has been worn away more quickly than the rock.

WHEN ROCKS BREAK UP

Rocks on Earth's surface are broken down by the weather. This process is called weathering. Rain dissolves some of the rocks. The Sun's heat makes the rocks swell a little and crack. Rainwater freezes in the cracks, and the ice pushes on the sides and breaks up the rock.

EROSION

The pieces of broken rock are washed away by the rain or blown by the wind. This moving away of the rocky fragments is called **erosion**.

It is not just the weather that can cause rocks to break up. The pounding waves of the sea have worn down and cracked these rocks over millions of years.

SEDIMENTARY ROCKS

Tiny grains of rock that have been washed away by the rain settle downriver in lakes and seas. When rock grains settle underwater they form **sediment**.

The grains of sediment pile up to form a layer. In time, the layer gets thicker and thicker. It gets so thick that it is squashed by its own weight. This turns the rock grains into a layer of solid rock. All rocks which have formed from layers of grains are called sedimentary rock.

Sand grains have settled to form these layers of a sedimentary rock called sandstone.

DESCRIBE ONE WAY IN WHICH THE WEATHER CAN AFFECT ROCKS.

ROCKS FROM LIVING THINGS

Some sedimentary rocks form from the shells of living things that lived in seas millions of years ago. When the creatures died, their empty shells settled on the sea floor and formed a layer which eventually turned into rock.

LIMESTONE

Limestone is a rock made from the shells of sea creatures, such as snails, clams, and crinoids, that lived millions of years ago. It can contain **fossils**!

A crinoid is a marine animal that has feeding arms and a stalk that secures it to the bottom of the sea.

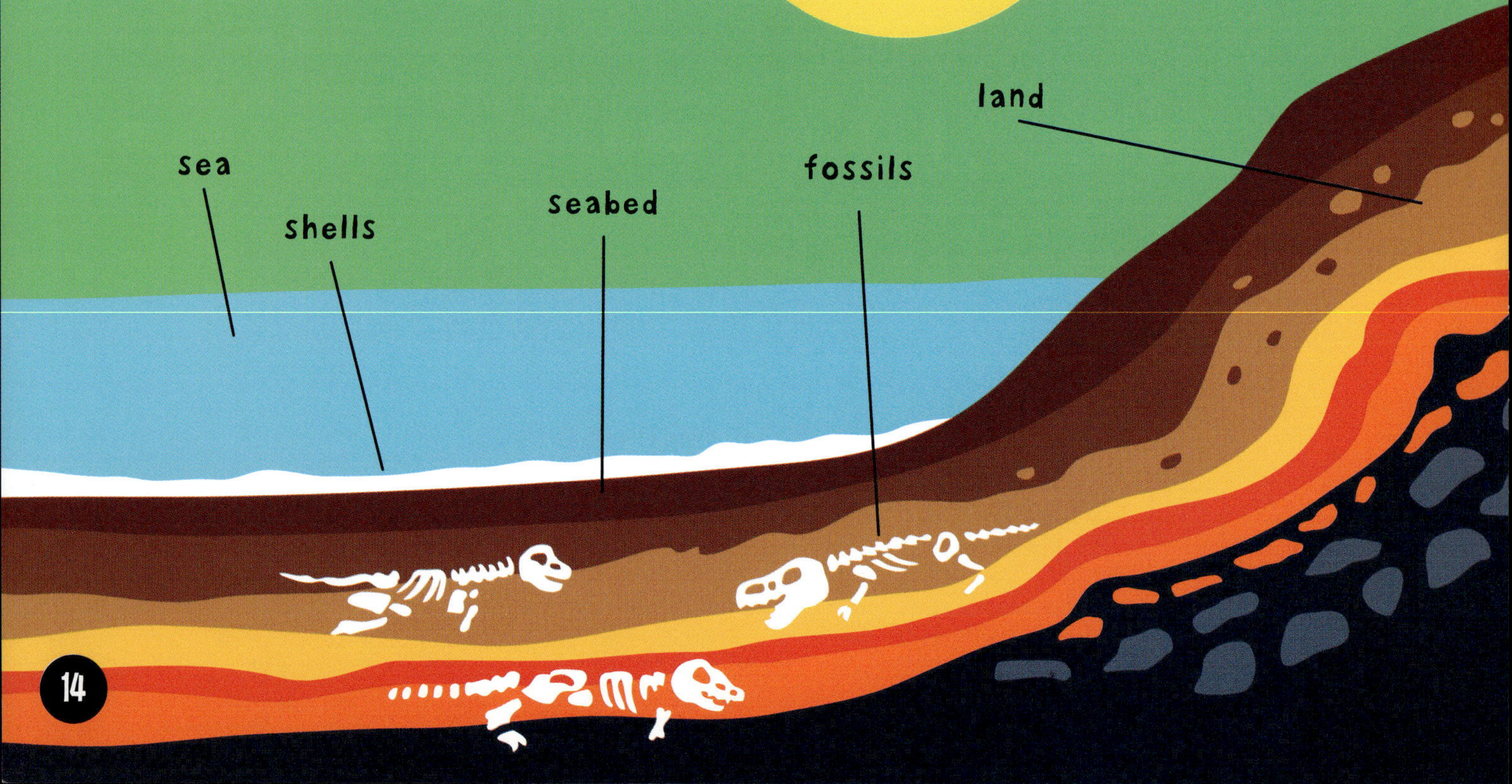

COAL

Millions of years ago, there were huge **swamps** on the Earth. Massive plants grew in them. When the plants died, they fell into the swamps. Over time, the plants turned into a hard, black rock called coal.

Today, coal is dug out of the dried-up swamps and burnt in power plants to make electricity.

CHALK

Chalk is a soft, white rock. It is a kind of limestone, which means it comes from the shells of sea creatures that lived millions of years ago.

DESCRIBE HOW CHALK IS DIFFERENT FROM COAL.

MINERALS

All rocks are made of minerals, which are made from chemical elements in the ground that link together and can form crystals. The crystals have different shapes, such as hexagons, and come in a variety of colors. They join together to form many kinds of rocks.

GEMSTONES

Some minerals are colorful, and some sparkle. These minerals are called gemstones. They can be used to make jewelry. In a diamond, a chemical element called carbon links together to make a hard, clear crystal. Diamonds are so strong they can be used to cut hard materials.

A geode is a hollow rock in which large crystals are formed.

These rocks containing diamonds have been discovered inside a mine.

MINERAL CRYSTALS

In most rocks , you cannot easily see the minerals' separate crystal shapes because they are locked together, making the rocks hard and strong. Some mineral crystals, such as calcite, are so small you can only see them with a **microscope**. The shells of sea animals are made from calcite. This makes the shells hard, protecting the animal inside.

You can see large crystals in granite. Granite is made from a pink mineral called feldspar, a black mineral called mica, and a white mineral called quartz.

METAMORPHIC ROCK

Metamorphic rock forms from another type of rock. Heat and pressure inside Earth's crust can cause a rock to change. For example, this happens when two tectonic plates in Earth's crust push together to form mountains.

Inside mountains, the Earth's plates push together, making the rocks change.

SLATE

Shale is a sedimentary rock. Its mineral crystals are locked together in all directions. When Earth's plates push together, the increase in heat and pressure makes these minerals change and line up in rows. This change creates a new, waterproof rock called slate. Slate is a hard rock which can be used in buildings for roof and floor tiles.

This **sculpture** of a lion has been made from marble.

MARBLE

Sometimes magma flows up inside cracks in the crust. It heats the rock next to the cracks and changes it. When magma heats limestone, it changes it into a metamorphic rock called marble. Marble is a very hard, smooth rock that can look sparkly like sugar. The clay and sand mixed in with the limestone change, too, making colored lines in the marble called veins.

SOIL

Soil forms from rock and living things. Wind, rain, and ice break down rock into sand, silt, and clay through erosion. The remains of dead plants and animals are broken down by bacteria, insects, and other living things to form humus. Humus mixes with the sand, silt, and clay and gives the soil its dark color.

RICH WASTE

Manure from animals can help form humus in the soil. Gardeners and farmers use manure to help plants and crops grow.

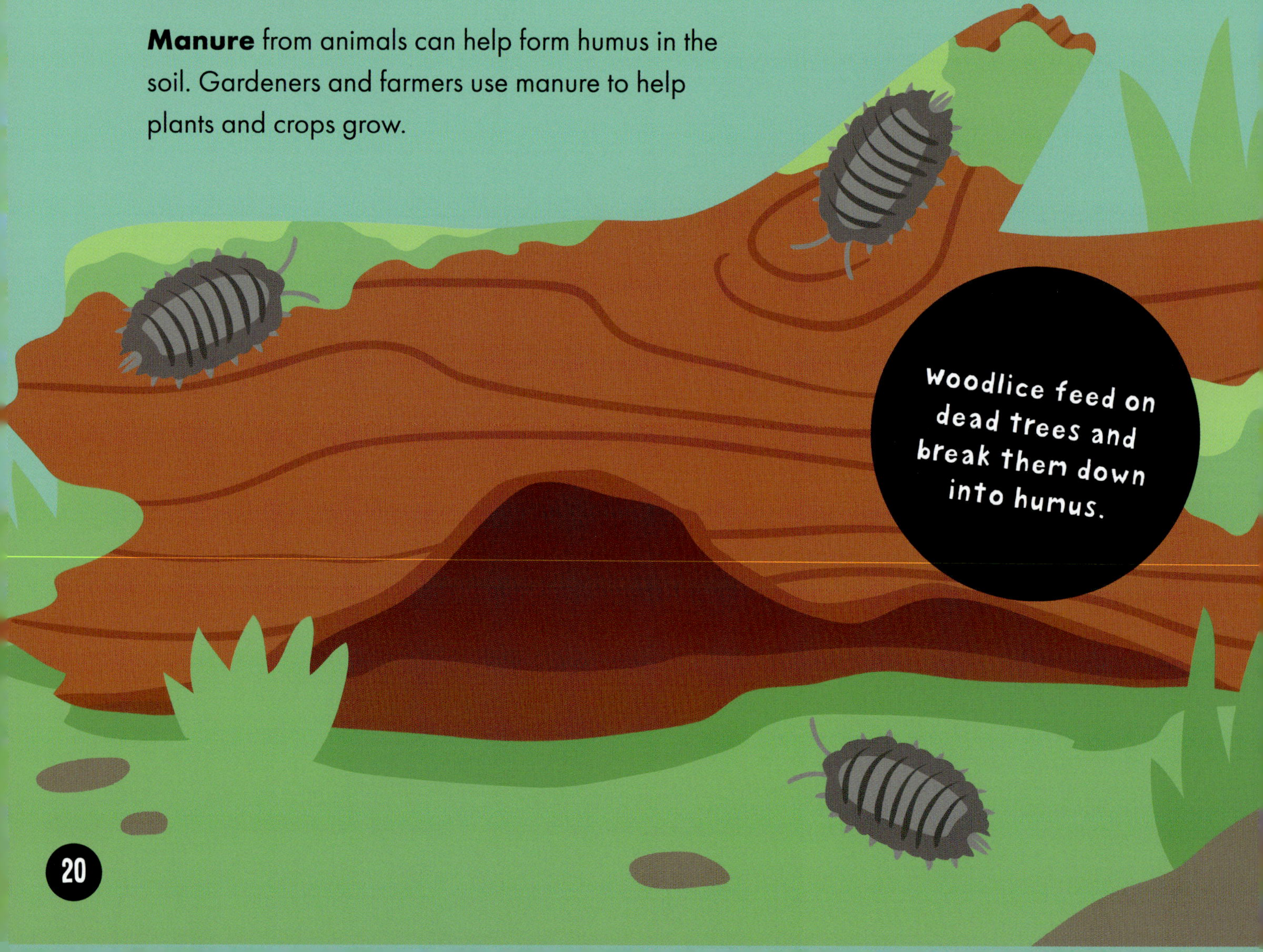

There are different types of soil:

SANDY SOILS

Sand particles are large and have big air spaces between them. Water can move through these spaces quickly and drain away.

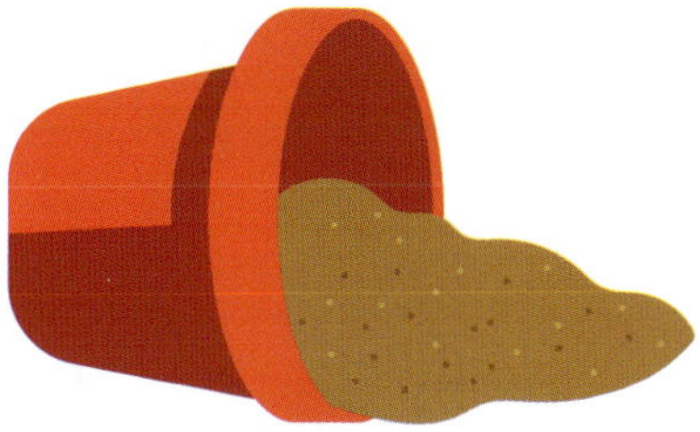

CLAY SOILS

Clay particles are very small and have very small air spaces between them. Water cannot pass through these spaces quickly and is held back above the soil.

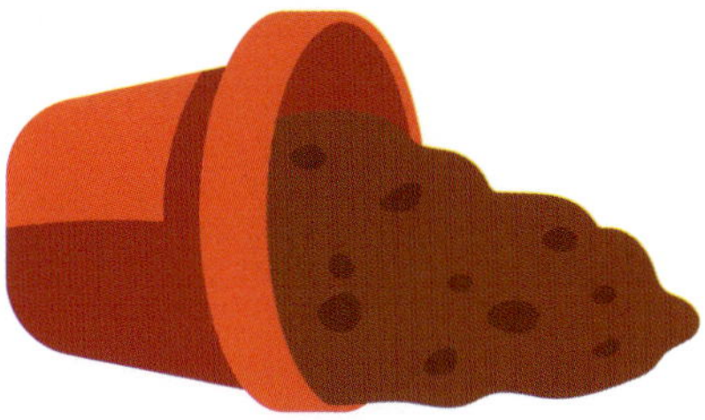

LOAM SOILS

Loam is a soil with a mixture of humus, sand, silt, and clay. The humus binds the rocky particles together to make large crumbs which help the soil drain well.

Gardeners use loam soil for growing plants.

DO YOU THINK LOAM HAS SMALL OR LARGE AIR SPACES? EXPLAIN YOUR ANSWER.

INVESTIGATING SOIL

Blue and Yellow have two samples of soil that they examine with magnifying glasses. They see soil A has larger particles than soil B. Yellow says soil A will have larger air spaces between the particles and so it will drain water faster than soil B. Blue and Yellow decide to test Yellow's idea. You can test it too!

EQUIPMENT:

- 2 types of soil (A and B)
- 2 funnels
- stopwatch
- cotton balls
- 2 plastic bottles (same size)
- water
- 2 graduated cylinders
- an adult to help

1 Yellow and Blue make a little plug with cotton balls in each funnel and place each funnel in the top of two plastic bottles.

2 Yellow and Blue put the same amount of soil in each funnel.

3 Blue pours the same amount of water into each funnel while Yellow starts the stopwatch.

4 After a set time, Yellow and Blue pour the drained water into their graduated cylinders to compare.

YELLOW SAID THAT SOIL A WOULD DRAIN WATER FASTER THAN SOIL B. WAS YELLOW'S IDEA CORRECT?

HOW FOSSILS FORM

Fossils are formed from animals and plants that lived long ago. When these animals and plants died, they were quickly covered with sand or mud. This stopped other living things from feeding on them and breaking down their bodies to form humus.

THE EFFECT OF WATER

Over time, the sand and mud turned into rock. Water passing through the rock dissolved some of its minerals. When the water reached the hard parts of the buried plant or animal, the minerals became solid again. They turned the hard parts of the dead animals and plants into fossils.

FINDING FOSSILS

Sometimes **trace fossils** form. Examples of trace fossils are animal tracks, dinosaur eggs, and the prints of leaves in a rock. The rocks above a fossil may be worn away by the weather. This uncovers the fossil and makes it easier to find. Fossils are collected by scientists who study them to find out about living things in the past.

This fossil has formed from a fish that died and was covered with sand. The sand settled over the fish and turned it to stone.

WRITE A STORY ABOUT A DINOSAUR BONE, FROM WHEN IT WAS IN THE LIVING ANIMAL TO WHEN IT WAS FOUND BY A SCIENTIST.

FOSSILS FROM DIFFERENT AGES

Fossils form in sedimentary rocks like sandstone and limestone. Over millions of years, layers of these rocks have been created in Earth's crust.

EARTH'S LAYERS

The oldest layers are the deepest, and the youngest layers are at the top. Each layer has been given a name, and scientists have worked out its age. Contained in each layer are many fossils. Scientists are able to tell the first time a type of animal or plant was present on Earth by the layer in which its fossil was found.

Name of layer	Time when the layer was made	Plant and animal fossils found
Quarternary	2.6 million years ago	First humans
Tertiary	65 million years ago	First **mammals**
Cretaceous	135 million years ago	End of dinosaurs
Jurassic	205 million years ago	First birds, first flowering plants
Triassic	250 million years ago	First dinosaurs
Permian	300 million years ago	Many **amphibians** and **conifer trees**; end of trilobites
Carboniferous	355 million years ago	First **reptiles**, first insects with wings, many ferns
Devonian	410 million years ago	Many fish, first amphibians
Silurian	435 million years ago	First centipedes and millipedes
Ordovician	510 million years ago	First **corals**, first land plants
Cambrian	570 million years ago	**Trilobites**, first **mollusks**
Precambrian	Before 570 million years ago	**Microbes** and **sponges**

EXTINCTION

Some fossils appear in older layers but not in newer layers. This means that the plants or animals that made them have died out, or become extinct. The dinosaurs became extinct at the end of the Cretaceous period.

Small sea creatures called trilobites became extinct at the end of the Permian period, over 250 million years ago.

EVOLUTION

Fossils show how one kind of living thing can change into another. For example, scientists believe that some ancient fish changed slightly every time a new fish was born. Over millions of years, these changes created the first amphibians. The first fish fossils appear in older layers, while the first amphibian fossils appear in younger layers. This changing of living things over long periods of time is called **evolution**.

GLOSSARY

Amphibian an animal, such as a frog, that lives both on land and in water but must lay its eggs in water.

Asteroid a piece of rock that moves around the Sun like the planets in the solar system.

Bacteria tiny living things which belong to a group called microorganisms or microbes.

Billion a thousand million.

Chemical element one of many different substances made up of only one kind of atom that come together to form all matter.

Conifer trees trees with long green needles that grow cones to make seeds.

Coral small animals that exist as polyps that live together and make tubes of hard rock around themselves.

Core the center of an object such as a planet or a fruit.

Crust the outer layer of rock on Earth which forms Earth's surface.

Crystal a solid with the atoms arranged in a way that makes the sides flat and forms shapes such as cubes or oblongs

Dissolve to go through process by which a solid breaks up into tiny pieces in a liquid and seems to disappear into it.

Erosion the breaking up of rocks into smaller pieces by the weather or ocean waves.

Erupt to let out magma and gases from inside Earth through an opening in Earth's surface.

Evolution a process in which living things change over a very long time.

Extinct no longer living on Earth or no longer active.

Fossil the remains of a plant or animal that have turned into stone.

Gas a substance which does not have any shape and can spread out but can also be compressed. It is not a solid or a liquid.

Grain a very small piece of rock such as a grain of sand.

Granite a rock that forms inside Earth's crust which is made of feldspar, mica, and quartz.

Gravel a small piece of rock.

Humus a dark, spongy substance in the soil that is formed from the decomposed remains of plants and animals.

Igneous a rock that forms from magma.

Lava magma that flows away from volcanoes and cools to form solid rock.

Liquid a substance that takes up the shape of its container and can flow from one place to another.

Magma molten (extremely hot) rock which forms in the mantle of Earth.

Mammal an animal with a backbone and hair which feeds on milk from its mother.

Mantle a layer of slowly moving hot rock below Earth's crust.

Manure the solid waste produced by animals that is used to help plants grow.

Metamorphic describing something that changes from one form to another.

Microbe one of a group of very tiny living things, also known as microorganisms.

Microscope a scientific instrument which makes objects appear bigger.

Mineral a solid that forms in the ground from elements that link together, often forming crystals.

Mollusk an animal with a soft body, with no legs, and which often has a shell, such as a snail.

Moon a large, usually round object which moves around a planet.

Particle a very small piece of a solid.

Planet a large, round object which moves in an orbit around the Sun or another star.

Reptile a land animal with skin covered in scales.

Sculpture an object made by carving rock or wood.

Sediment a layer at the bottom of a liquid which forms from tiny solid particles that were floating in it.

Solar system the Sun and all the objects that orbit around it.

Sponge an animal which stays in one place and draws water in through the tiny holes in its body to help it feed.

Star a huge ball of gases that gives out heat and light.

Swamp a piece of land soaked with water, often found next to a pond or lake.

Trace fossils fossils made by a plant or an animal, like a track or print.

Trilobite an extinct animal that looked like the woodlice we see today.

Volcano an opening in Earth's crust which releases lava, rocks, and hot gases from inside Earth.

ANSWERS TO THE ACTIVITIES AND QUESTIONS

Page 5: Rocks in Space

Answer: The planets Mercury, Venus, Earth, and Mars are made out of rocks. Asteroids are made out of rocks, as are moons.

Page 11: Igneous Rock

Answer: Basalt and granite are similar because they both come from hot rock under the Earth's crust. Basalt and granite are different because basalt comes from lava that has flowed away from a volcano and is black. It is made from tiny grains packed together. Granite forms in the crust and is made of crystals.

Page 13: When Rocks Break Up

Answer: It breaks up the rock into tiny pieces called fragments and scatters them in the wind or washes them away in rainwater.

Page 15: Rocks from Living Things

Answer: Chalk is a white rock made from the shells of living things that were in the sea long ago. Coal is a black rock made from plants, which fell into swamps millions of years ago but did not fully break down.

Page 21: Soil

Answer: It has large air spaces. Sand particles are large, and sandy soil has a lot of air spaces. Crumbs are also large soil particles, so they will also have large air spaces between them.

Page 23: Investigating Soil

Answer: Yellow's idea is correct. You can see from the measuring cylinders that the one collecting water from soil A contains more water than soil B.

Page 25: How Fossils Form

Here is an example of a story about a dinosaur bone: The dinosaur died. It fell into mud and was quickly covered up with more mud as a river flowed over it. Over time, the mud hardened into rock. Water passing down through the rock dissolved some of the minerals, but when they reached the dinosaur bones, the minerals solidified inside the bones. More time went by, and the rocks above the dinosaur bones were worn away by the weather. The dinosaur bones stuck out of Earth's surface. A scientist then found them.

FURTHER INFORMATION

BOOKS TO READ

Earth's Amazing Cycles: Rocks by Jillian Powell, Franklin Watts

The *Geology Rocks* series by Izzi Howell and Claudia Martin, Wayland

Science Skills Sorted!: Rocks and Fossils by Anna Claybourne, Franklin Watts

WEBSITES

This informative site has useful animations about the rock cycle.

min4kids.org

This website features facts about minerals.

www.ducksters.com/science/earth_science/minerals.php

This article breaks down the basics of geology, which is the name for the scientific study of rocks.

kids.nationalgeographic.com/science/article/geology-101

NOTE TO PARENTS AND TEACHERS:

Every effort has been made by the publisher to ensure that these websites contain no inappropriate or offensive material. However, because of the nature of the internet, it is impossible to guarantee that the content of these sites will not be altered. We strongly advise that internet access is supervised by a responsible adult.

INDEX